COOL CAREERS
WITHOUT COLLEGE
FOR PEOPLE WHO LOVE
FASHION

COOL CAREERS
WITHOUT COLLEGE
FOR PEOPLE WHO LOVE
FASHION

ALISON DOWNS

ROSEN
PUBLISHING®

New York

Published in 2017 by The Rosen Publishing Group, Inc.
29 East 21st Street, New York, NY 10010

Copyright © 2017 by The Rosen Publishing Group, Inc.

First Edition

Library of Congress Cataloging-in-Publication Data

Names: Downs, Alison, author.
Title: Cool careers without college for people who love fashion / Alison Downs.
Description: First edition. | New York : Rosen Publishing, 2017. | Series:
  Cool careers without college | Audience: Grades 7 to 12. | Includes
  bibliographical references and index.
Identifiers: LCCN 2016018582 | ISBN 9781508172789 (library bound)
Subjects: LCSH: Fashion design—Vocational guidance—Juvenile literature. |
  Fashion merchandising—Vocational guidance—Juvenile literature. |
  Fashion—Vocational guidance—Juvenile literature. | Clothing
  trade—Vocational guidance—Juvenile literature.
Classification: LCC TT507 .D596 2017 | DDC 746.92/023—dc23
LC record available at https://lccn.loc.gov/2016018582

Manufactured in Malaysia

CONTENTS

INTRODUCTIC

Do you spend hours skimming through fashion magazines, scouring fashion websites, and watching shows like *Project Runway*, *RuPaul's Drag Race*, and *What Not to Wear*? If so, you've probably already considered a career in fashion. If you are wondering where to start or have been discouraged by a reportedly high barrier to entry, this book is the perfect solution for you. Inside, you'll find real-life examples from others just like you who chose fashion over college.

If a career in fashion feels like the right one for you, it's not that difficult to begin your career. The fashion industry may seem endlessly glamorous, but it's really not all that hard to break into—you don't need to be born into the right family, live in a big city, or have a college degree in order to make your mark. If you love shopping, have a killer sense of style, and know your way around a sewing machine, you're already on your way. If you have some basic retail or customer service skills, that's even better.

Models walk the runway during Idan Cohen's show at New York Fashion Week. Cohen is one of Israel's most celebrated bridal and eveningwear designers.

College decision time may be looming in the distance, but you might not be as pumped about it as some of your friends. Maybe you don't have the funds to go to college, you have responsibilities at home that won't allow you to leave, or maybe you've just never really cared for school in the first place. Whatever the reason, it's OK to opt out of college if you have a good career path in mind. If you know what you want to do and you're truly dedicated to achieving your goals, college isn't always your only option.

In the following chapters, you will learn about ten different jobs within the fashion industry—everything from costume designing to public relations work. Some you may have never considered before! None of these careers require you to have a college degree in order to be successful, but don't misunderstand—just because these jobs might not necessarily require a degree doesn't mean that they are easy! Each job requires hard work and dedication. Some may require long hours, late nights, or a lot of time spent on your feet. But the best thing about these jobs is that they are accessible. They're not a pipe dream, even though a lot of people might say just the opposite. You can make them a reality with a little bit of hard work and dedication.

Each entry in the following chapters describes the job in detail and explains the training or skills you may need, while also providing you with lots of resources for gaining more information or getting started. You'll even find valuable interviews from people already working in the fashion industry! Many of these jobs listed can be worked as a second job, allowing you to gain valuable experience while still being able to pay the bills.

Whatever your current situation, it is possible to have a career in fashion without a degree, and many people have already done so. Read on to find out how you can get started!

CHAPTER 1

INDEPENDENT DESIGNER

Maybe you carry around a thick sketch-book that is filled with sketches of elaborate outfits and accessories or you can't walk past a clothing rack without examining the cut of a garment closely: running your finger along the stitching, pulling on the fabric. You love your sewing machine so much, you actually have a relationship with it … and your significant other is starting to get jealous. When people compliment you on your outfit, you're likely to respond, "Thanks, I made it myself." On the weekends, you can often be found at thrift stores, grabbing high-quality vintage pieces and tailoring them to fit a more modern silhouette. You love skimming magazines and catalogs, and you have notebooks full of outfits that inspire you. If this sounds like

Sketching out clothing designs is a great way to nail down your concept before you actually begin designing—it allows for risk-free experimentation.

you, you might be interested in a career as an independent designer.

A DAY IN THE LIFE

Sketching out outfit ideas, shopping for fabric, and becoming well acquainted with dress dummies of various sizes are all par for the course for the average designer. You'll be your own boss, mostly, so you're in charge of scheduling your tasks in the order that makes the most sense to you. For example, if you're slow to get going in the morning, you may choose to spend your morning hours sipping coffee and answering customer e-mails, placing online orders, making phone calls, or checking out your competition. Once you're more awake, you can move on to physical errands: picking up materials, working on patterns, measuring, cutting, and sewing. You might even schedule special events during the weekend, like pop-up shops or photo shoots. You're busy, productive, customer focused, and you

Study the work of designers you admire closely. What do you like about their pieces, and what elements do you think you could improve upon?

13

always keep an eye out for your next opportunity. You may work from home, from a coworking space, or from a small studio that you've rented.

WHAT EDUCATION AND TRAINING DO INDEPENDENT DESIGNERS NEED?

If you plan on taking care of your business on your own, you'll need to be proficient with a sewing machine and know your way around a computer in order to start an online shop. Some knowledge of social media platforms will be helpful, and Facebook, Twitter, and Instagram are good places to start. You might want to look into some tax courses for small business owners, too.

To begin, you may want to start small—posting your finished pieces to an Etsy shop or taking on custom work. It might take a while for you to find a niche. Once you've been working like this for some time and you have built up a small group of followers and clients, you may want to expand by taking your designs to small boutique stores in your area. Show them that you have a following and present your best-selling designs to them. They may take some pieces on consignment on a trial basis—meaning they pay you based on what sells, and you take back the items that don't. If your pieces are successful, this is a good way to build a relationship with boutiques.

Etsy is a great way to begin selling your pieces, but it's also a wonderful research tool when it comes to keeping tabs on your competition.

Always keep an eye out for free business workshops and networking opportunities in your area. Your public library is a great resource, and your local chamber of commerce is another. Soak up all the insider knowledge you can get. It's important to make sure you have all necessary legal permits and documentation, and small business workshops can help

HOW TO SET UP YOUR FIRST ETSY SHOP

Setting up an Etsy shop is quick and easy! First, you'll need an account at Etsy.com. It takes only a few minutes to set one up, and from there, you can choose a shop name, open your shop, and begin selling!

If you haven't already chosen a name for your shop, take some time to really think about this … it's more important than you might realize! Ask friends for help if you need to. You want a name that is catchy, clear, and unique. It should have some personality, and above all, your shop name should describe your shop! For example, "Diana's Delightful Designs" may have alliteration going for it, but the shop could be selling anything! Try something like "Diana's Delightful Dresses" instead.

Setting up the account is the easy part; it's setting your business apart from the competition that is more difficult. How will you market your products? What makes you different from other designers out there? Etsy offers a variety of tutorials and guides to help you take the most effective product photos, how to best word your posts, and more. Poke around and check out what some successful shops are doing. Learn from them, but don't copy them.

with that. Don't get tangled up in red tape before you even get your business off the ground!

You'll also want to read all you can get your hands on when it comes to the world of fashion design. Can you accurately describe the difference between an A-line dress and a dress with an empire waist? Do you know what culottes are? What about gaucho pants? Fashion tends to be cyclical, so make sure you study fashions of yesteryear as well as modern fashions.

It's also important to remember that Instagram users are very influential these days. Keep your eyes peeled for a blogger whose style you admire, who you think might like your designs. Go ahead and send him or her some shirts or a dress—something that matches the blogger's style. Tell the blogger that you'd love it if he or she would wear it in a photo and tag you in it.

SALARY EXPECTATIONS

You'll need some money up front in order to start an enterprise such as this. If you don't have a hefty savings account to pull from or family that could donate money to help your cause, you may have to apply for a small business loan or rely on angel investors in order to get things started. If you have a lot of supportive friends and family, it might be worth it to start a Kickstarter or Indiegogo campaign.

Your salary will depend entirely on your profits. Some days you might have a windfall, and sometimes you might feel the pinch. It's rare for small businesses to turn a profit until the second or third year, so you might want to have another source of income when you first get started. Remember not to get frustrated if big things aren't happening right away—these things take time. Remain patient and dedicated to your business, keep your quality up, and focus on keeping your customers happy and eventually things will start to come together!

CAREER OUTLOOK

Fashion design is a very competitive field. There are more than one million independent designers on Etsy already.

Once you've been selling clothing for a while, you may find that the quality of your workmanship has improved drastically or that you now find yourself drawn to higher -quality fabrics. If this is the case, you can increase your prices a bit to make up the difference in cost. You can also reach out to other designers (or you may find that other designers are reaching out to you!) and work on a collaboration. Whatever you do, keep making contacts and forming positive relationships with everyone you work with. If you see an opportunity to help someone out, do so … and don't be afraid to ask for help if you need it, too.

FOR MORE INFORMATION

BOOKS

Burns, Leslie Davis, Nancy O. Bryant, and Kathy K. Mullet. *The Business of Fashion: Designing, Manufacturing, and Marketing*. New York, NY: Fairchild Publications, 2002.
This textbook covers everything from the history of textiles to how to distribute your products. A valuable resource!

Gehlhar, Mary, and Diane Von Furstenberg. *The Fashion Designer Survival Guide: Start and Run Your Own Fashion Business*. New York, NY: Kaplan, 2008.
This book is packed with real-world examples and lots of tips from industry experts. If you're aiming for high fashion, this is a good reference.

Stewart, Briana, and Brian Cliette. *Clothing Line Start-up Secrets: How to Start and Grow a Successful Clothing Line*. CreateSpace, 2014.
An intro into the business side of launching your own line. If you aren't sure where to start, this resource has you covered.

Wolff, Colette. *The Art of Manipulating Fabric*. Radnor, PA: Chilton Book, 1996.
If you thought all there was to sewing was stitching two pieces of fabric together, think again! Wolff sets you straight in this detailed look into sewing techniques.

ORGANIZATIONS

Council of Fashion Designers of America (CFDA)
65 Bleecker Street, 11th Floor
New York, NY 10012
Website: http://cfda.com
This organization provides links to professional
    development opportunities, as well as a database full
    of production facility resources.

International Association of Clothing Designers and
Executives (IACDE)
Susan Nickel
Freudenberg Nonwovens LP
New York, NY 10018
Website: http://iacde.net
This organization welcomes young entrepreneurs that
    want to learn from the best of the best in the industry.

United Stages Fashion Industry Association (FIA)
1140 Connecticut Avenue, Suite 950
Washington, DC 20036
(202) 419-0444
Website: https://www.usfashionindustry.com
Founded in 1989, USFIA is a great resource if you're
    looking for information on trends, regulations,
    and requirements.

WEBSITES

Because of the changing nature of internet links, Rosen Publishing has developed an online list of websites related to the subject of this book. This site is updated regularly. Please use this link to access this list:

http://www.rosenlinks.com/CCWC/fash

CHAPTER 2

COSTUME DESIGNER

Do your friends call you the king of cosplay? Do your skills include whipping up a killer costume practically overnight, while also knowing how to get stains out of any fabric—fast? Do you love art and culture? If your idea of a good time is attending a convention or a Broadway show or you loved watching fashions change over time on *Downton Abbey*, you may really enjoy the behind-the-scenes life of a costume designer!

A DAY IN THE LIFE

As a costume designer, you have a variety of choices to choose from. You might work in theater, television,

You might have only considered cosplay as a hobby, but the skills you learn while making your costumes could be the springboard for a whole new career!

Curator Jemma Conway adjusts the jewelry on one of the Dowager's elaborate costumes from *Downton Abbey*; the costumes will be on exhibition in the Cannon Hall Museum, England.

print, or film, so a day in the life will vary from assignment to assignment. For a television job, you might spend a while reading a script, talking with directors, and forming a lookbook for the characters you are dressing—or you may be responsible for the wardrobe of a large group of extras.

Do you love scouring thrift stores for the perfect designer find or vintage conversation piece? Great, because a huge part of being a costume designer involves finding those costume pieces you've just dreamed up in your lookbook! Costume designers often spend long hours at thrift shops, shopping malls, costume shops, and the like, digging through dusty bins. You might need to locate a chicken costume one day and ten pinstriped suits the next— so if you don't love shopping and don't live for the thrill of the hunt, this job might not be for you. You'll need to work within a budget, too, so being a savvy shopper who is good with numbers (or knows how to negotiate in order to get a bargain!) helps.

Research, research, research! A costume designer should be able to tell you exactly what a crinoline is and during which time period people often wore one. Don't worry if you don't have the answers right now, but be prepared to brush up on things like that, depending on the project you're working on. A costume designer on the *Downton Abbey* set, for example, should be eagle-eyed and able to jump in and correct any wardrobe snafus before anyone else notices.

Sketching designs, shopping for fabrics, cutting, sewing, and pinning—these are other tasks that will make up the majority of a costume designer's day! You might make costumes from scratch or spend large chunks of your time scouring antique shops for vintage finds.

WHAT TRAINING DO COSTUME DESIGNERS NEED?

You don't need to be an expert seamstress in order to work as a costume designer. "I was a shopgirl in clothing and jewelry stores, and the experience I gained while working with the general public is what most effectively prepared me—because dressing people is really all about sales. I paint a picture with words and images that allows people to believe in me and see what the end result will be," Alison Freer, fashion designer and author, says in her book *How to Get Dressed: A Costume Designer's Secrets for Making Your Clothes Look, Fit, and Feel Amazing.*

If you're in high school, costume design is perhaps one of the easiest jobs in which to gain experience! High school drama clubs tend to put on anywhere from two to four stage

Costume designers can often be found behind the scenes at photo shoots and on film or television sets, making sure every outfit looks just right.

productions each year, and they frequently need help of all kinds ... including wardrobe help! Show up ready to roll up your sleeves—a short-staffed crew will be happy to have you.

If your high school drama club isn't an option, take a look in your local paper for acting troupes in your area for some (likely unpaid) on-the-job training. At first, you might only shadow another wardrobe manager—fetching costume

FIVE COSTUME DESIGNERS YOU SHOULD KNOW

There are plenty of talented costume designers in the industry. Some have already left us, and some are just emerging. It's a good idea to become well versed in the legendary costume designers—here are just a few to get you started!

Edith Head – In the world of costume design, Head currently holds the record for the number of Oscars, clocking in wins for *The Sting, The Facts of Life, Sabrina, Roman Holiday, A Place in the Sun, All About Eve, Samson and Delilah,* and *The Heiress.* She styled such superstars as Audrey Hepburn and Natalie Wood, and she even has her own star on the Walk of Fame on Hollywood Boulevard.

Colleen Atwood – A frequent collaborator with Tim Burton, Atwood has styled *Alice in Wonderland, Edward Scissorhands,* and *Ed Wood,* as well as the showstopping *Chicago,* for which she won an Oscar.

Eiko Ishioka – Responsible for the ornate designs in films like *The Cell, Dracula,* and *The Fall,* Eiko Ishioka worked as a costume designer, art director, and graphic designer. The *New York Times* called her the "costumer of the surreal."

Janie Bryant – If you loved the amazing vintage-style pieces used on AMC's *Mad Men* (and how could you not? They were fabulous!), you'll need to get better acquainted with Janie Bryant. In addition to her television work, she's also collaborated with brands such as Maidenform and Banana Republic.

FOR MORE INFORMATION

BOOKS

Beckett, Nicole. *The Fantabulous Girl's Guide to Wardrobe Styling: How to Break into the Fashion & Entertainment Industry*. Amazon Digital Services, 2015.
A great resource if you're looking specifically to break into television, film, or commercial styling, industry veteran Beckett offers tips she's gleaned from her twenty years on the job.

Freer, Alison. *How to Get Dressed: A Costume Designer's Secrets for Making Your Clothes Look, Fit, and Feel Amazing*. Emeryville, CA: Ten Speed, 2015.
A guide that grabs you from the first page, Freer sprinkles personal anecdotes in with pearls of wisdom. A must read if you like a side of sass with your style.

Ingham, Rosemary, Liz Covey, and Arvin Brown. *The Costume Designer's Handbook: A Complete Guide for Amateur and Professional Costume Designers*. Portsmouth, NH: Heinemann Educational, 1992.
Though a bit dated, this is possibly the costume designer's most valuable resource, teaching you how to research a play and how to design for characters. Very handy and full of reference lists!

ORGANIZATIONS

American Association of Community Theater
1300 Gendy Street
Fort Worth, TX 76107-4036
Website: http://www.aact.org
If you're under eighteen, you can sign up
  for a membership for only $10 a year. This
  membership gains you access to conferences
  and workshops, discounts, a bimonthly
  magazine, and more.

Costume Designers Guild
11969 Ventura Boulevard, 1st Floor
Studio City, CA 91604
Website: http://costumedesignersguild.com
This organization is concerned with improving
  working conditions for designers. It also
  features a member directory, awards, and many
  other resources.

National Costumers Association
PO Box 3406
Englewood, CO 80155
Website: http://www.costumers.org
This organization offers a quarterly magazine,
scholarships, and more.

WEBSITES

Because of the changing nature of internet links, Rosen
Publishing has developed an online list of websites
related to the subject of this book. This site is updated
regularly. Please use this link to access this list:

http://www.rosenlinks.com/CCWC/fash

CHAPTER 3

PR ASSISTANT

If you've already done the blogging thing and know how to build your brand, great! If you've even done some fashion writing for magazines and know how to write a clear, concise pitch, even better! Are you a whiz at social media, too? That's just the icing on the cake. If you love fashion but don't necessarily want to design it, fashion public relations (PR) is a great field worth looking into.

A DAY IN THE LIFE

Consider this situation: You're a vegan and you love animals. They aren't exactly haute couture, but would you purchase a pair of UGG boots? The answer here is most likely no, and that's probably

One part writing, two parts networking, a career in PR can be hard work, but it's also fun and rewarding!

because you've heard the rumor—or seen the awful video—that a lot of us have: that UGG removes sheepskin when the sheep are still alive. But a quick search of the UGG website proves that this rumor is exactly that … a rumor. "UGG® only uses animal hides that are a byproduct of another industry," the UGG website claims, which means that sheep are slaughtered for their meat first, then UGG acquires the sheepskin. (Still not ideal for a vegan, obviously, but preferable.)

The point of this story is that if there are some who still think UGG skins live sheep, that means that the UGG PR team needs to work a little bit harder to change perceptions.

PR teams are in charge of making sure their company's reputation remains uncluttered; if something happens to

Imagine you are a PR representative for UGG. During what season might you select this photo for an ad campaign? What sort of text would you run with the image?

AN INTERVIEW WITH BRITTANY SANFILIPPO, AN INTERN AT A PR FIRM.

Is it safe to say PR is basically social media marketing's big sister?

Yes, that's exactly what it is! It's making a brand cool and keeping it cool. Some [PR] agencies only focus on getting publicity for the products, and some also have their hands in sales. It's key to build relationships within the industry; this is how you get bloggers and editors to come to the showroom to pull samples from your client's collection.

Publicists can also create pitches to send to editors and bloggers that would include pieces of their client's collections. Additionally, PR agencies can host press days or fashion shows where they invite editors, bloggers, and possibly even buyers; it's a way for industry press to learn about your clients and preview their upcoming collections for future pulls. A fashion show is pretty much the same thing, except it is normally for one collection at a time and involves production at an outside venue. Sometimes public relations companies host other promotional events as well and are involved with celebrity dressing. On a day-to-day basis, you are keeping track of samples, gathering press clips, vetting contact lists, keeping track of appointments for pulls, [and] writing press releases and pitches. That's sort of what fashion PR involves, in a traditional sense. Today, most agencies also offer social media and digital services to their clients; that involves sometimes creating lookbooks and line sheets. It also could be creating blog content or across-the-board social media.

Continued on page 38

Continued from page 37

What tips would you offer to young people wanting to get into the industry?

If you are interested in fashion and your school has fashion, art [or business] courses, take them! It is important to understand how art and business collide. Stay on top of the most current social media trends and also be conscious of what you post on social media. Use the internet to your advantage; you can learn a lot and find a lot of opportunities. The Fashion Institute of Technology offers precollege courses. Take every opportunity you can to get one step closer to your dreams; don't tell yourself you can't just because you are in high school. I think it's important to break out of your comfort zone and take control of your future. Think about your personal brand and what you want to represent. Network as much as possible, [and] start thinking about internships.

Tell me a little bit about your experience at Fashion Week!

I can't tell too much. That's important to realize in fashion … there are definitely some trade secrets! What I can say is that if you want to work Fashion W eek, be prepared to work. You have to leave the diva at the door and be professional. Many people think that working in fashion is extremely glamorous. Some parts of it are, but it definitely is not all the time. It's a lot of work. You have to be able to keep your cool around celebrities—there are a ton roaming around at Fashion Week. It is important to stay professional.

Can you recommend any texts on fashion PR?

Women's Wear Daily is key to learn what is going on in the industry. It is also important to keep up with the most popular blogs and fashion magazines. A book that really set the record straight for me was *Leave Your Mark* by Aliza Licht; she basically changed the game when it came to social media for fashion brands. Her book has a lot of advice about résumés, cover letters, internships, and first jobs.

tarnish it, the PR team comes in to straighten things out the best they can. To put it simply, public relations assistants work to keep companies in the public eye in a positive way.

Sometimes companies take care of their own PR in-house, and sometimes they hire PR agencies to take care of their reputation and promotion for them. A PR agency has many clients, which can be useful when it comes to forming connections within the industry.

WHAT TRAINING DO YOU NEED?

Before going in for your first PR interview, you should already have a strong interest in fashion and some insider

Many skills can translate into a PR job, so think outside of the box when writing up your resume. If you interviewed people during your time with the A/V club, include that!

knowledge about how the industry works, so read up! If you have some experience with media—for example, writing for your high school paper; helping out a friend with content for their Facebook, Instagram, or blog; or even running cameras at a local cable access channel—that will help your résumé look a little more attractive.

SALARY EXPECTATIONS

The average salary for a PR assistant will vary from company to company. For more specific figures, refer to the Bureau of Labor Statistics website.

CAREER OUTLOOK

Good news! The PR sector is experiencing average growth. So finding and keeping a job in public relations shouldn't be too difficult. You might choose to start out as a PR intern— you may even be able to intern while you're still in high school, if your school allows it—and look for PR assistant jobs once you're finished. If you don't mind getting your feet wet in nonfashion PR, it shouldn't be hard to find a job. If you're looking for fashion PR only, you may want to focus your job search on large metropolitan areas.

FOR MORE INFORMATION

BOOKS

Licht, Aliza. *Leave Your Mark: Land Your Dream Job. Kill It in Your Career. Rock Social Media*. New York, NY: Grand Central Publishing, 2015.
A fun, quirky romp with the former "DKNY PR girl," this book gives a unique inside look at the world of PR.

Noricks, Crosby. *Ready to Launch: The PR Couture Guide to Breaking into Fashion PR*. CreateSpace Independent Publishing Platform, 2012.
A straightforward reference that gives you insight into the world of fashion PR.

Sherman, Gerald J., and Sar S. Perlman. *Fashion Public Relations*. New York, NY: Fairchild, 2010.
This textbook-like reference book is chock-full of practical tips and real-world examples.

ORGANIZATIONS

Fashion Institute of Design and Merchandising
919 South Grand Avenue
Los Angeles, CA 90015
(800) 624-1200
Website: http://fidm.edu

The alma mater of Lauren Conrad, FIDM has summer courses for high school students in addition to standard college classes.

Mastered
6-8 Hemming St.
London, England E1 5BL
Website: https://www.mastered.com
If you're looking to hone your skills, Mastered offers a writing course aimed at fashion journalists.

Public Relations Society of America
33 Maiden Lane, 11th Fl.
New York, NY 10038-5150
Website: https://www.prsa.org/index.html
This organization provides a great way to stay on top of emerging trends while also making contacts in the PR industry.

WEBSITES

Because of the changing nature of internet links, Rosen Publishing has developed an online list of websites related to the subject of this book. This site is updated regularly. Please use this link to access this list:

http://www.rosenlinks.com/CCWC/fash

CHAPTER 4

FASHION BLOGGER

Tavi Gevinson was a tiny twelve-year-old with a killer sense of style when her fashion blog—*Style Rookie*—first started gaining momentum. Now, she's the editor in chief of the magazine *Rookie*, a writer, actress, and singer. Of course, these results aren't typical, but fashion blogging can bring you lots of perks!

Update regularly, be authentic, and build up a good following, and you're bound to be getting business inquiries left and right. Up-and-coming companies are usually eager to find influential bloggers who can tout their wares.

A DAY IN THE LIFE

Have you ever heard the saying "you get out what you put in"? That's particularly true in the world of blogging: how dedicated you are to your blog will determine the sort of rewards you reap. You can keep a 9–5 job and blog sporadically on the side, but you might miss out on some

Since hitting it out of the park as a style blogger, Tavi Gevinson has stepped away from the fashion world. Currently she focuses more on pop culture and feminist discussion.

INTERVIEW WITH FASHION BLOGGER KENDRA L. SAUNDERS

What made you want to be a fashion blogger?

Fashion was a world that was very far apart from me as a child and teenager, both due to a very conservative upbringing and because the industry seemed to be accessible only for the thinnest, prettiest, richest people in the world. As I got older, I began to view fashion more as an art form, something that can be appreciated, as much for as in spite of, its impracticality. I came to appreciate the exaggerated aspects of fashion, from bold colors to oversized shapes, to outrageous accessories. It wasn't until the rise of fashion blogs that I realized there are countless other people like me out there: people who enjoy the artistry and unmatched glamour of fashion. I realized I wanted to make a blog that is positive, accessible, and full of good advice for the WHOLE body, not just what goes on it. That desire to host a size/body inclusive blog really became a cause dear to my heart. Since then, I've looked at my role as a blogger to be one of bringing joy and glamour to EVERYONE. That's what keeps me going!

How do you stay up-to-date in the fashion world?

I've been a fan of *InStyle* magazine for ten plus years; their viewpoint is one of unabashed love for fashion, so I definitely try to keep up with them. I also enjoy *Cosmopolitan* as a prompt for

Continued on page 46

InStyle magazine was founded in 1994 and holds the distinction of being the first monthly fashion magazine to feature famous actors or musicians on the cover.

Continued from page 45

women's issues in pop culture, and I love *Glamour* for all things makeup and styling. I watch *Project Runway* almost every week!

Instagram is a great place for keeping up with fashion and makeup trends, so I check that many times a day. A few Instagram accounts I really like are @marielfip, @rosiehw, @creationsbyelina, and @_illnanax3.

As for websites and blogs, WWD.com holds almost everything fashion related in one spot, which is incredible. Fashionista. com is also great, and *Vogue*'s website is a great resource during

Fashion Week—they always have the best photos of everything the runway has to offer.

What are the benefits of being a fashion blogger?

Currently [my] blog is set up to accrue earnings from ads over time. Many other bloggers make decent money from their ad placement. For me, the benefit lies more in access to events, getting to have conversations with people in fashion whom I admire, and receiving feedback from people who enjoy the blog's positive, accessible spirit.

important fashion events in the process, be slow to respond to comments, or not spend as much time on promotion or outreach as is necessary.

A fashion blogger doesn't just live a life of luxury while occasionally blogging. You'll need to hustle: if companies aren't contacting you, you'll need to reach out to them, introduce yourself, and make connections. Some days you might need to write guest posts on other prominent blogs to increase your readership; other times you may need to focus on improving your search-engine optimization, also known as SEO, and web rankings.

It's also important to build your brand and not stray from it. The tone of your posts should generally stay the same (if you're friendly, be friendly; if you're snarky, stay snarky), but you also want to keep your content fresh.

Make sure you're being consistent across platforms, too. Don't gush about the latest Prada line in your blog and then trash it on Twitter. Whenever you get ready to post online, ask yourself if it helps to perpetuate the personality of your brand. If not, reconsider what you're about to write.

WHAT TRAINING DO YOU NEED?

If you're a skilled writer, good with a camera, and don't shy away from interviewing people for articles, you already have all the skills you need to succeed.

It's a good idea to educate yourself on SEO best practices, and if you learn a little bit of HTML and Photoshop, you'll also be able to design your blog so it looks exactly how you want it to.

SALARY EXPECTATIONS

Once you start getting a lot of visitors to your site, you can begin to sell ad space. You can also optimize your site with various tools like Google AdWords and start earning revenue whenever your blog visitors click a sponsored link.

Being a fashion blogger means a lot more than taking selfies! Engaging, well-curated images are sure to keep your readers coming back for more.

There is no average salary for a fashion blogger—your success depends on how many people view your page. If you have a lot of visitors, large companies will take notice and reach out to you, offering to pay you in exchange for talking about their products.

CAREER OUTLOOK

Companies always need brand ambassadors to help introduce others to their products, and bloggers are great in this regard. At first, fashion bloggers might be gifted with items in exchange for a post, rather than monetary payments—a few articles of clothing to try on for a photo shoot or a ticket to a fashion event, for example. As your readership grows, however, so will your rewards.

One of the great things about being a fashion blogger is that you can literally blog from anywhere. So what if you live out in the country, miles away from a Target, let alone a Nordstrom? If you have a computer, an Internet connection, and a little determination, you can still make things happen.

FOR MORE INFORMATION

BOOKS

Hayward, Sarah. *Fashion Blogging: How to Become a Superstar Fashion Blogger*. Lion Day, 2015.
If you're looking for a quick and simple read, you can usually find this text on Amazon for not much money. It's great if you're looking for a basic overview before starting out.

Swanson, Kristen K., and Judith C. Everett. *Writing for the Fashion Business*. New York, NY: Fairchild, 2008.
This text is required reading for quite a few fashion degree programs—and with good reason! Read up on the business side of blogging … but don't expect any tips on social media from this 2008 edition; it's a bit dated in that respect.

Ziv, Yuli. *Fashion 2.0: Blogging Your Way to the Front Row: The Insider's Guide to Turning Your Fashion Blog into a Profitable Business and Launching a New Career*. Lexington, KY: CreateSpace, 2011.
A guide that has been called the bible for fashion bloggers, Yuli Ziv interviews popular bloggers and writes about her own experiences.

ORGANIZATIONS

A Beautiful Mess
137 Park Central Square
Springfield, MO 65806
Website: www.abeautifulmess.com
Run by sisters Elsie and Emma, this website is equal parts
    style blog, craft blog, and classroom. Swing to check
    out their "Sister Style" posts, and take a look at their free
    blogging and photography tips... you may even want to
    enroll in an online course while you're there!

Independent Fashion Bloggers
824 Henderson Road
Hood River, OR 97031
Website: http://heartifb.com
This is a community that supports fashion bloggers.
    Become a member to get access to eCourses,
    photography tips, and more.

International Blogger Association
PO BOX 193
Elizabethtown, KY 42702
Website: http://www.internationalbloggersassociation.com
With a tagline like "let's make your blog awesome," it's
    easy to see why this is a helpful resource for newbies

and seasoned pros alike! Although it isn't a fashion-focused organization, there are lots of great how-to articles and useful guides.

WEBSITES

Because of the changing nature of internet links, Rosen Publishing has developed an online list of websites related to the subject of this book. This site is updated regularly. Please use this link to access this list:

http://www.rosenlinks.com/CCWC/fash

CHAPTER 5

FASHION WRITER

If you love fashion, have strong opinions, and have a way with words, becoming a fashion writer is a natural next step. Different from a fashion blogger, a fashion writer submits stories to magazines or newspapers rather than posting them on his or her own platform. While a fashion blogger might write posts about his or her top five favorite trends of the moment, a fashion writer will instead pitch numerous article ideas or work on assignment, perhaps shadowing a designer or attending a fashion event.

Some fashion writers, like critic Robin Givhan of the *Washington Post*, have advanced degrees in journalism—but writing is a field in which a strong portfolio can sometimes trump a degree.

Although fashion writers generally need to meet tight deadlines, the good news is that there is usually some flexibility when it comes to location. Writers can work wherever there is a Wi-Fi connection!

Do you have proof of your awesome writing chops? Can your references vouch for your ability to meet tough deadlines and go that extra mile? Polish up your portfolio, make sure it's accessible online, and get ready to wow some editors!

A DAY IN THE LIFE

A finger on the pulse of current events is crucial: as a fashion writer, you will have to know what (and who!) is hot now—and it's even better if you can predict trends before they hit!

As you first start out, this might mean you are glued to award shows like the Oscars, describing what the latest "it girl" is wearing, or you might review up-and-coming independent brands, or interview independent designers. These gigs can generally be done from home at first. After a while, you might be asked to cover larger events, such as fashion shows or product launches … that sounds a little more exciting, doesn't it? Like with any job, you'll need to prove yourself before you get involved in the fun stuff!

WHAT TRAINING DO YOU NEED?

If you're already a solid writer, you're halfway there! If you're a so-so writer, don't worry, there's still hope for you. First, work on honing your skills—take a creative writing class, a journalism class, a literary theory class, a publishing class…

Being a fashion writer means you sometimes need to write elaborate text about somewhat nondescript images. Can you write an engaging paragraph about this model's outfit?

HOW TO PITCH A STORY

Let's face it, no matter how great your portfolio is, the odds are that most fashion editors won't be banging down your door asking you to write for them. You'll need to have fresh ideas, seek out gigs, and pitch your ideas to editors.

When pitching an article, you should first ask yourself a few questions:

Is this story relevant and timely? It's always best when you can tie your article to a current event. No one cares about what Kate Winslet wore to the Oscars two years ago. They care about what she wore *this* year.

Why am I the best person to write this article? This can be hard to answer, especially considering you can't just say, "because it's my idea and you can't have it." Try to tie yourself to the work personally. If you're a fashionista who wears plus-size clothing and Melissa McCarthy's label Seven7 just released its spring line, that's enough of a personal intersection!

Is my article the right style for this magazine? Study magazines closely before you pitch an article. Make sure that your style of writing and your topic both fit well with this magazine. Is this something you could see their readers being interested in? Make sure they haven't published a similar article within the past few months, too. This required research doesn't need to be expensive—libraries often carry magazine back issues, so definitely take advantage of them.

HOW TO PITCH

Find the e-mail address of the magazine you want to submit to and send off a quick "prepitch" e-mail. In this e-mail, introduce yourself and summarize the main points of the article you wish to submit. Ask if they'd like to see the pitch. Be friendly but professional.

Write the pitch. A pitch should be no longer than a page. Editors are busy people, so it's best to keep things short and sweet whenever possible. Paste your pitch into the body of an e-mail—no attachments! Only send attachments if editors specifically ask for them.

Write the article while you're waiting for a response. If the editor likes your pitch, he or she will ask to see more. If the editor doesn't like your pitch, you can move on and pitch the idea to someone else!

Tweak your article as needed. Always keep the voice of the magazine in mind—you may need to edit your article if you submit it to different places.

whatever you can get your hands on. If you haven't already, start a blog. Look for writing groups in your area and ask for feedback on how to make your work even stronger. Step out of your comfort zone as much as possible. Volunteer to write articles for your school newspaper, or try to snag an

There are many classes available that can help you hone your writing skills and develop your "voice!" Take advantage of any courses you can find, and be sure to network with your colleagues there.

internship at your local rag. If all else fails, read … a LOT. Subscribe to fashion magazines and pay particular attention to the style the authors use. Don't neglect online magazines, either.

You'll also need a selection of clips (writing samples) to send out when you're applying— most places request two or three samples. When you're first starting out, you might find yourself taking some unpaid assignments. Working for free is the pits, but sometimes you need to get some published clips before other, more exclusive magazines will take you seriously. If you do find yourself working for free, ask yourself two questions: is this helping my career and am I gaining anything from this?

Invest in a tape recorder (or make sure you have a recorder app on your phone) and learn to take notes quickly and efficiently. Learning shorthand isn't really necessary, but make sure you can decipher your own notes.

SALARY EXPECTATIONS

If you're looking to find work as a full-time fashion journalist or writer, refer to the Bureau of Labor Statistics website for the most up-to-date salary figures. If you plan on doing some freelance writing on the side, however, your pay can vary. Some magazines don't pay their writers at all, some pay a flat rate for each assignment, and some pay per word.

CAREER OUTLOOK

You can be a fashion writer from anywhere in the world, but it might help if you at least live near a major city—or can travel frequently.

While the field is competitive, fashion writers are always necessary.

FOR MORE INFORMATION

BOOKS

Benson, Chris, and Charles F. Whitaker. *Magazine Writing*. Florence, KY: Taylor & Francis, 2014.
Learn best practices that will help you launch your career as a magazine writer.

Ruberg, Michelle. *Writer's Digest Handbook of Magazine Article Writing*. Cincinnati, OH: Writer's Digest, 2005.
This text starts out with the basics but continues way beyond that, even covering rights issues and other frequently asked questions.

Swanson, Kristen K., and Judith C. Everett. *Writing for the Fashion Business*. New York, NY: Fairchild, 2008.
This text is required reading for quite a few fashion degree programs—and with good reason! Read up on the business side of blogging … but don't expect any tips on social media from this 2008 edition; it's a bit dated in that respect.

ORGANIZATIONS

American Society of Journalists and Authors
355 Lexington Avenue, 15th Floor
New York, NY 10017-6603
Website: http://www.asja.org/index.php
A great way to make connections within the journalism
industry.

Editorial Freelance Association
71 West 23rd Street, 4th Floor
New York, NY 10010
Website: http://www.the-efa.org
Offers many resources—like sample contracts and
invoicing examples—that are useful for freelance
writers who are just starting out.

The National Writer's Union
256 West 38th Street, Suite 703
New York, NY 10018
Website: https://nwu.org
A valuable resource for writers, providing contract
assistance, press passes, and more. Dues are paid on a
sliding scale, which helps to keep the cost reasonable.

WEBSITES

Because of the changing nature of internet links, Rosen Publishing has developed an online list of websites related to the subject of this book. This site is updated regularly. Please use this link to access this list:

http://www.rosenlinks.com/CCWC/fash

CHAPTER 6

FASHION PHOTOGRAPHER

Are your friends always handing you their phones and asking you to take the perfect new profile photo? Have your art teachers told you that you have a "good eye" for composition, detail, color, or use of light? Do you shrug at your friend's updates on Facebook and Twitter but live for the more dynamic images of Snapchat and Instagram? If you answered yes to any of these, you might consider a career behind the camera as a fashion photographer.

A DAY IN THE LIFE

A photographer's day will look drastically different depending on the project she is working on. One day, she could be in the studio, setting up lighting and backdrops, then shooting pairs of sparkling high heels, one right after the other; the next day she could be on a beach in the dead of winter, taking photos of a freezing model in a bikini. The day after that, she might be covering Fashion Week. The possibilities are endless!

Photography might look fun and easy, but it's actually a lot of work and requires sacrifice and dedication. Don't sign on unless you're ready to take it seriously.

WHAT TRAINING DO YOU NEED?

Some high schools offer photography courses, and if yours does, you should definitely sign up and take notes! You're sure to learn a thing or two about composition, digital editing, and maybe even dark room developing!

To be a good photographer, you should definitely know your way around cameras, both SLR and DSLR. Know the difference between ISO and aperture; know what different lenses are for and how to change them. A good photographer rarely shoots in manual mode, so don't allow yourself to rely on it! You should be a pro when it comes to composing a good shot and also have a good eye for color and texture … knowing how to use Photoshop and Lightroom is a big plus!

Once you're confident, reach out to photography studios in your area and ask if they need any help. Shadow some studio photographers, offer your services as an intern, and send photos to your local paper or news outlet. Many independent coffee shops will allow photographers to hang and sell their work, but sometimes there is a long waiting list.

SALARY EXPECTATIONS

Fashion photographers make better rates in larger cities, but it's not unheard of for fashion photographers to live in rural

BILL CUNNINGHAM AND STREET STYLE

Bill Cunningham (1929–2016) was perhaps the poster child for how you don't need a college degree to be a successful fashion photographer. Born in Boston, Cunningham dropped out of Harvard University and instead went to work in advertising. First working as a writer for the *Chicago Tribune*, Cunningham made substantial contributions to fashion journalism, working for *Women's Wear Daily*. Eventually he wound up at the *New York Times*, where he wrote two columns.

Bored by celebrities, Cunningham preferred to shoot people on the streets of New York, showing how they use fashion as they go about their day. This has resulted in hundreds of charming "street style" photographs. Usually found riding the city streets on his bicycle, Cunningham was a quiet, unobtrusive force, snapping photos of anyone he found interesting. Later, he analyzed the photos for eye-catching details and common themes. In the fashion industry, being photographed by Cunningham was considered a huge honor.

areas. For a better idea of current salary figures for photographers, refer to the Bureau of Labor Statistics website.

You may need to take some smaller photography jobs as you work your way up to working in fashion. Make sure you give each job your all!

CAREER OUTLOOK

When you get a few great images under your belt, you can try your hand at selling prints and making some money on the side. You must make sure your models have signed proper release forms, though. Many photographers list their prints on Etsy.com, but you can attempt to sell them wherever you have a large following. Did your photo get one thousand likes on Instagram? Make sure your followers know they can purchase it for themselves! Photographers seem to have a great deal of luck on Tumblr, so make sure you don't neglect that platform.

Check out SmugMug.com and Fine Art America, where you can easily create an account and upload your photos. The websites allow customers to buy prints, greeting cards—even duvet covers and tote bags that feature your art. You don't have to worry about making the prints or shipping out purchases; that's all taken care of for you.

You can be a photographer anywhere—people will always need someone to take their modeling headshots, family photos, and senior pictures. But to be a great fashion photographer with a busy career, ideally, you should live near a big city.

Although smartphones can take some impressive photos these days, you aren't going to impress anyone if that's all you shoot with! Invest in a decent camera.

FOR MORE INFORMATION

BOOKS

Jade, Lara. *Fashion Photography 101: A Complete Course for the New Fashion Photographer*. London, England: Ilex, 2012.

Take a peek behind the scenes as Lara Jade shows you what equipment is best, how to pick models, and how to arrange and execute a photo shoot.

Remy, Patrick. *The Art of Fashion Photography*. New York, NY: Prestel, 2014.

A collection of cutting-edge fashion photography ideal for anyone interested in high fashion.

Siegel, Eliot. *Photographing Women: 1,000 Poses*. Berkeley, CA: Peachpit, 2012.

A great resource to study before you begin shooting models, this book showcases a variety of poses for when you're not sure what to do next.

ORGANIZATIONS

American Photographic Artists
2055 Bryant Street
San Francisco, CA 94110
Website: http://apanational.org

Enjoy essential business references, information on liability insurance, and even discounts on Apple products by signing up.

American Society of Media Photographers
150 North Second Street
Philadelphia, PA 19106
(215) 451-2767
Website: http://asmp.org
This organization offers seminars, webinars, and allows you to find a local chapter so you can connect with other industry professionals.

Professional Photographers of America
229 Peachtree Street NE, Suite 2200
Atlanta, GA 30303
(404) 522-8600
Website: http://www.ppa.com
This organization was created by professional photographers and continues to be run by them. Benefits include networking opportunities and malpractice protection.

WEBSITES

Because of the changing nature of internet links, Rosen Publishing has developed an online list of websites related to the subject of this book. This site is updated regularly. Please use this link to access this list:

http://www.rosenlinks.com/CCWC/fash

CHAPTER 7

FASHION MODEL

If you love to strut your stuff as much as you love fashion, there's a good chance you'd enjoy being in the spotlight. Whether you're walking the runway at New York Fashion Week or posing for editorials, you're sure to be wearing only the hottest new trends.

A DAY IN THE LIFE

If you think modeling is easy, think again! Days are long and often involve tons of walking, standing in uncomfortable shoes, and facing casting directors—which can sometimes result in a lot of rejection. This is one job within the fashion industry that definitely requires a thick skin, as your appearance is on the line. Someone might

The best accessory is a great complexion, so it's important for models to keep their skin healthy. Make sure to take off your makeup every night and drink lots of water.

No matter what part of the fashion industry suits your career needs, you'll need to have a portfolio that showcases your accomplishments. You can even create an online portfolio, rather than the traditional physical one.

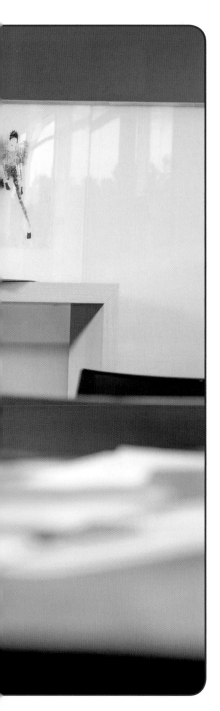

not like your nose, and poof! That's enough reason for you to be out of a job. You'll need to have the where-withal to hold your head up high and realize that your nose is fine just the way it is and another casting director is searching for a nose just like yours.

WHAT TRAINING DO YOU NEED?

If you're already poised and expressive, you might not need much training at all. The best thing you can do to prepare for your career is to perfect a selection of poses. Compile an outstanding portfolio that will set you apart from the crowd.

Work to build your self-esteem, if necessary, and work on developing a thick skin. As a model, you're being judged based on your appearance alone, and sometimes you simply don't fit the casting director's vision. This can be frustrating and sometimes even insulting. You'll have to try to not take it personally, which can be difficult.

Models also need to keep fit, do their best to keep their skin clear, and maintain good posture. If you don't already have one, look into a good skin care regimen and make sure you're following a healthy lifestyle when it comes to food and diet.

SALARY EXPECTATIONS

Modeling is much like acting and writing. At first, you will probably manage to scrape by with odd jobs here and there that don't pay much. Early on in your career, you might need to find another job in order to make ends meet. The goal is to sign with an agency, which will then work to get you larger and more frequent jobs.

There are many different ways to model, and there are thousands of working models in the world—it's important to be realistic and to remember that you won't likely become the next Kate Moss or Heidi Klum. Like with any job, though, it's important to make connections and earn a reputation for your hard work and dedication. Set your sights high, but don't think yourself "above" any job—unless it's something that makes you uncomfortable. Definitely don't accept jobs that make you feel uncomfortable.

AN INTERVIEW WITH MODEL MADISON THIBODEAU

How did you get involved in modeling?

I never wanted to model. When I was fourteen, my friend asked to use me for a photo shoot for a local clothing brand, [but] I said no. My parents weren't pleased with the idea of a young boy shooting me. [But then] he showed me [his work]. [The model] was dressed, looked comfortable, and it looked pretty good for just a start, so I agreed to let him use me. As I was in front of the camera with the fan going and music playing, something just sparked for me.

How did your career change after being signed by an agency?

Before the agency, I had little to no deals or serious connections and now I have the opportunity to meet and get to know some incredible people. I finally am getting my face and name out there. Life is definitely a lot easier with an agency.

What was it like to walk the runway during Fashion Week?

When I booked my shows for Fashion Week, I didn't realize that I was actually going to be *in* Fashion Week. It was so exciting. Hitting the runway was the best feeling I've had modeling thus far. It's like the fifteen minutes of fame again, but it's [actually] only fifteen seconds! I had such an adrenaline rush and I wanted to go again and again. The show was only ten minutes long, but all the preparation and the angst were so worth the moment when I hit the runway.

Continued on page 82

Continued from page 81

You chose modeling over college. What advice would you have for someone in high school who wants to follow in your footsteps?

Don't feel pressured to follow what society says if you know in your heart it's not what you want. If you know what you want and can envision your life being something greater than what school says they'll offer, then just do it. For young aspiring models, stay true to who you are. Learn and stick to your passion and really go for what you want. Have patience; that is something I'm still learning every day. Nothing happens overnight.

Sure, a gig modeling for stock photography websites might not seem very glamorous … but at least it's a job. Take it until another one comes along.

CAREER OUTLOOK

As long as the fashion industry exists, there will be a need for models. There can often be a great deal of competition (once you attend your first casting, you'll see evidence of this when you see the long line of models waiting to be seen), but the good news is that the job

Kimora Lee Simmons's mother enrolled her in modeling classes at the age of eleven in order to help build her self-esteem. By the age of fourteen, she had signed an exclusive contract with Chanel.

forecast seems steady. For more specific and up-to-date salary information, refer to the Bureau of Labor Statistics website.

Sometimes modeling can lead to an unexpected career opportunity. For example, former model Kimora Lee Simmons (who, by the way, doesn't have a college degree) wound up serving as the creative director of the clothing line Baby Phat, eventually getting promoted to president and creative director of Phat Fashions.

FOR MORE INFORMATION

BOOKS

Goss, Judy. *Break into Modeling for Under $20*. New York, NY: St. Martin's Griffin, 2008.
A straightforward reference that some call the only book on modeling you'll ever need. Learn how to take photos, promote yourself, and what to say at your first agency interview.

Lane, R. C. *The Model's Bible*. CreateSpace, 2013.
This insiders' guide offers a look into different types of modeling, castings, and more.

Sigel, Eliot. *Photographing Women: 1,000 Poses*. Berkeley, CA: Peachpit, 2012.
If you want to model but aren't sure what to do in front of this camera, let this book be your guide. It features a huge variety of poses to add to your wheelhouse.

ORGANIZATIONS

Elite Model Look
19 Avenue George V
75008 Paris, France
Website: https://www.elitemodellook.com/int/en/home/index.htm

Elite Model look is considered the most prestigious modeling contest in the world, and it's where models like Cindy Crawford and Gisele Bundchen got their start.

Model Alliance
302 A West 12th Street, Suite 136
New York, NY 10014
Website: http://modelalliance.org
A labor group that works to stand up for models' rights and to give models a voice.

World Model Association
34 rue de l' Athenee, CH-1206
Geneva, Switzerland
Website: http://www.worldmodel.org
This group matches models with modeling agencies, talent scouts, and photographers worldwide.

WEBSITES

Because of the changing nature of internet links, Rosen Publishing has developed an online list of websites related to the subject of this book. This site is updated regularly. Please use this link to access this list:

http://www.rosenlinks.com/CCWC/fash

CHAPTER 8

FIT MODEL

Don't let the name fool you—"fit model" isn't short for "fitness model." Also called a fitting model or a try-on model, a fit model actually is in the middle of the fashion process. A fit model tries on clothes after they're designed and created but before they are released to the public.

The point of a fit model is so that designers can see how the garments hang on a real person, rather than a dress dummy or a hanger. Do the sleeves hit at the right point? Are the shoulders too narrow? A fit model would be the one to help a designer figure this out.

If you are fairly proportionate (and your proportions stay somewhat consistent year-round—if you put on some extra "winter weight" around the holidays and have trouble losing it, this job might not be for you), you might be the right choice for a brand. A big perk of this job is that you'll get to see the new fashions before anyone else.

Some people love the thrill of trying on a new outfit and admiring themselves in front of the mirror. If you are one of those people, fit modeling would be a great job for you!

A DAY IN THE LIFE

Sometimes you may be asked to complete a variety of administrative tasks, but most of the time you'll be trying on clothes. There's no room to feel bashful, though, as you'll most likely be walking around in Spanx-type undergarments in between wardrobe changes. While dressed, prepare to feel a little invisible as coworkers poke and prod at the outfits you're wearing, making sure the quality, fit, and appearance are up to par.

You'll need to be able to accurately describe how the article of clothing feels on you, too, so get ready to be descriptive. Move around in the garment; treat it the same way you would if you were trying it on in a store. Can you comfortably sit in those pants, or do they pull too tightly, causing too much stress on the seams?

The range of motion you have when wearing a particular article of clothing is extremely important, especially for a fit model. You'll want to be able to move normally.

COULD YOU BE A FIT MODEL?

As you've no doubt realized by now, clothing sizes are inconsistent and may vary from brand to brand. A size six dress by Calvin Klein might fit more like an eight from another designer, while a Kate Spade six could be more like a four.

Because of this, where you'll "fit" as a fit model is different from company to company. The first thing to take into account is your height. Are you average height, tall, or petite? Next, take an objective look at your size. Do you wear juniors clothing, or is your body type a bit wider, like misses or plus size? Take your measurements and determine where you fit. Take your measurements several times over the course of a month; this will help you to determine a more accurate range. These are the measurements you will send out to agencies. If your measurements are within the range of a clothing line, you will be contacted.

There's no easy way to tell if you might be a perfect fit model. Sometimes companies use padding so that a size eight model can accurately model a size ten dress. The only way to know if you might be a good fit model is to apply and find out. Good luck!

As a fit model, any shyness you have about your body needs to be left at the door. You'll be measured and touched constantly, so it's important that you are comfortable with that.

Button up that blazer and attempt to shake someone's hand—do you have a full range of motion? How does the fabric feel against your skin? If the fit is awkward, be clear as to why.

WHAT TRAINING DO YOU NEED?

Not much! Depending on the company, you might need to answer phones, take messages, and do some light filing, so customer service or secretarial experience might be helpful.

This is a great gig for models who may not necessarily meet the more strict measurement requirements for print and runway. If you're a female under five feet eight inches (173 centimeters) tall, for example, you might have a hard time finding runway work. However, petite fit models are often needed.

Discerning taste might be helpful, too. If you try on a lot of clothing but rarely buy because things aren't up to your standards, you might be a great fit model.

SALARY EXPECTATIONS

The average salary for a fit model appears to be higher than that of a print model, but this may vary from company to company or campaign to campaign. For a complete updated list of salary information, refer to the Bureau of Labor Statistics website.

CAREER OUTLOOK

As long as there are clothing companies, there will be a need for fit models. Designers always need to know exactly how their clothing hangs on certain sizes. However, a quick search shows that fit models are most in demand in New York City and Los Angeles. If you don't already live within commuting distance of these cities, it might be difficult to find work.

FOR MORE INFORMATION

BOOKS

Goss, Judy. *Break into Modeling for Under $20*. New York, NY: St. Martin's Griffin, 2008.
A particularly helpful reference that offers some insight into working with an agency.

Lane, R. C. *The Model's Bible*. CreateSpace, 2013.
This insiders' guide offers a variety of advice—pay special attention to the chapters on working with an agency.

Siegel, Eliot. *Photographing Women: 1,000 Poses*. Berkeley, CA: Peachpit, 2012.
Though you won't necessarily be getting your photo taken as a fit model, except maybe now and again, look to this book for tips when it comes to posing. Your posture will affect how a garment looks.

ORGANIZATIONS

Fit Models LA
447 S. Robertson Boulevard #204
Beverly Hills, California 90211
(212) 490-1162

Website: http://www.fitmodelsla.com
Represents the "best production fit models in the heart of the fashion district." They also have a showroom and print division.

Fit Models LLC
124 E. 40th Street, Suite 1103
New York, NY 10016
Website: http://www.fitmodelsllc.com
Founded by a former Ford Models employee, Fit Models LLC also provides runway and print models and is the only agency that manages both plus size models and former male athletes.

MSAFit
200 W 41st Street, Suite 1000
New York, NY 10036
(212) 944-8896
Website: http://msamodels.com/la/Fit/be_a_fit_model
An offshoot of MSAModels. Apply to be a fit model simply by entering your measurements.

WEBSITES

Because of the changing nature of internet links, Rosen Publishing has developed an online list of websites related to the subject of this book. This site is updated regularly. Please use this link to access this list:

http://www.rosenlinks.com/CCWC/fash

CHAPTER 9

VISUAL MERCHANDISER

Visual merchandisers often have a "good eye" for fashion. They know how to put together an outfit that looks amazing and is perfectly suitable for any occasion; but more than just that, visual merchandisers have a good eye in general. They can walk into a store and instantly know when something is out of place or if something is positioned awkwardly. They might walk into your house and tell you how much space you'd gain if you moved your couch 3 inches (8 cm) to the right and kitty-corner to your coffee table.

If you love to make things look "just so," you might enjoy a career as a visual merchandiser.

You're at the mall for a pair of shoes—but those sunglasses in the window display catch your eye and draw you into the store. That's no accident; that's visual merchandising hard at work!

INTERVIEW WITH VISUAL MERCHANDISER KAREN CASTILLO

Why did you choose a career as a visual merchandiser instead of going to college?

I had a hard time knowing what to choose for a college career, [and] going to college can be way too expensive. I did [want] to do special effects makeup for movies, but looking at how much I had to pay for classes and how many jobs are actually available, it was just too much for me. Instead, I decided to get a job in retail.

What are some of your daily responsibilities?

Being a visual merchandiser is a lot of fun! I've always had an eye for art and being creative, [and] doing this job really opens your eyes to how putting a store together can be [similar to] painting a canvas. This job really consists of being creative with colors, shapes, and space. My days consist of making a map of our new merchandise for every new floorset. I get to learn about the colors that are in style, [and] I get to work with clothing, putting outfits together for our mannequins. Becoming the visual director for a store can also be stressful. There [are] times that we don't get everything, or we don't get enough to make the whole floorset how the company wants it, but that's when you become creative. You get to work with what you have and it's fun to show what you are capable of doing. After I'm done with the floorset, I send pictures of the store to be reviewed by headquarters. They give me feedback on how the store looks and how we can improve.

What is your favorite part of your job?

I get to see the new merchandise before anyone else! It's always fun to see the new products and know what my next purchase is (most of the time I want to buy everything). Also another great perk about the job is that I can show what I'm capable of doing. I get to be creative, learn about fashion, and read books that can help me improve in my art skills.

What skills should an employee bring to this job?

Like any job, you have to be passionate. Be able to work with colors, know how to pair colors, know the difference between warm and cool tones, understand complementary colors and patterns. Understand negative space—make sure that we [have] filled the wall, but it's not overwhelming to the eye. Also, [be] willing to take criticism. It's the only way you will improve in a field of fashion.

Do you have any advice to people who want to be a visual merchandiser?

Never stop learning. There are many books out there that will help you improve in this career. Most importantly, do it because you love it. Show your love for fashion and art, read magazines, and learn about trends. But most importantly make sure you love your job.

Many visual merchandisers start out as retail sales associates and are then promoted, so don't get discouraged if you can't find a visual merchandiser position right away.

A DAY IN THE LIFE

Visual merchandisers are responsible for creating eye-catching displays, which might involve dressing mannequins, posting signage, deciding what lighting looks best, and sometimes even painting walls or shelving.

They also are available to help guide both employees and customers when it comes to making the best outfit choices—in some luxury stores, they may even function as personal shoppers.

WHAT TRAINING DO YOU NEED?

Although there are many visual merchandising courses and books, training is frequently done on the job. Often, employees may begin as cashiers or customer service representatives and work their way up to becoming visual merchandisers.

A visual merchandiser dresses a mannequin with minimalistic accessories. You want all your elements to work together, not distract from each other.

If you want to become a visual merchandiser, it can be helpful to get your start in any retail establishment. Learning to work on a register and answer phones will be helpful, but the most important things you can learn are how to keep everything looking nice. Learn your store policy when it comes to "facing" or straightening, and take it to heart—making stores look presentable will be your bread and butter as a visual merchandiser.

SALARY EXPECTATIONS

The salary of a visual merchandiser can vary from store to store and state to state, but the pay is generally competitive. Go to the mall and take a look around. See those pretty displays? Proof that visual merchandisers are everywhere!

For more detailed and updated salary information, refer to the Bureau of Labor Statistics website.

CAREER OUTLOOK

This is one job in fashion that won't require you to move to a big city … you can be a visual merchandiser just about anywhere.

FOR MORE INFORMATION

BOOKS

Bailey, Sarah, and Jonathan Baker. *Visual Merchandising for Fashion*. New York, NY: Fairchild, 2014.
Take a look at some of the psychology behind why we shop the way we do.

Ebster, Claus, and Marion Garaus. *Store Design and Visual Merchandising: Creating Store Space That Encourages Buying*. New York, NY: Business Expert, 2011.
Learn the secrets that will make your displays stand out from the competition.

Pegler, Martin M. *Visual Merchandising and Display*. New York, NY: Fairchild, 2012.
Everything a visual merchandiser needs to know about displaying your items so that they sell.

ORGANIZATIONS

Association for Retail Environments
440 N. Wells Street, Suite 740
Chicago, IL 60654
Website: http://www.retailenvironments.org
Dedicated to "enhancing the total shopper experience," this association publishes educational information and also sponsors industry awards.

Footwear Distributors and Retailers of America
1319 F Street NW #700
Washington, DC 20004
Website: http://fdra.org
This group advocates for fair taxation in the industry, among
other things.

National Retail Federation
1101 New York Avenue NW
Washington, DC 20005
(800) 673-4692
Website: https://nrf.com
This organization represents a large variety of retail
establishments—everything from mom and pop shops to
luxury department stores.

WEBSITES

Because of the changing nature of internet links, Rosen
Publishing has developed an online list of websites related to
the subject of this book. This site is updated regularly. Please
use this link to access this list:

http://www.rosenlinks.com/CCWC/fash

CHAPTER 10

FASHION BUYER

Are you a trendsetter? Do others often ask where you got your clothes, only to come in the next day sporting something similar? If you love nothing more than helping your friends pick out a killer new outfit (and in fact, you know *just the thing* that will look fabulous on them), a career as an assistant buyer might be just the ticket.

A DAY IN THE LIFE

Unfortunately, the life of a fashion buyer isn't all fashion shows and photo shoots—but that's part of it. A typical day might consist of answering e-mails, placing orders,

Being a fashion buyer may mean communicating with clients or placing orders on the go; it's probably not the job for a homebody who doesn't like to talk on the phone.

scheduling photo shoots, and discussing garments. There's number crunching involved, too. You may need to keep track of how well your items are selling in retail establishments, perform market research, and stick to a budget when you're making purchases. You need to look at your budget and make sure that your business stands to make a profit from the items you're selling.

Lots of travel will be required, so having a car or at least knowing your way around your city's public transit system will be important.

Being a buyer is about more than ordering bright colors for spring and summer and dark colors for fall and winter. A buyer must intuitively know not only what colors will be popular for the coming season but what styles as well.

An eye for interior design may be helpful, too, as buyers are sometimes responsible for setting up displays in order to best exhibit their wares.

How are your people skills? It may be time to practice making eye contact, smiling, and actively listening.

WHAT TRAINING DO YOU NEED?

A background in retail and a love for fashion will help you to go far as a fashion buyer. If you know a bit about marketing and merchandising, you're well on your way, so look for entry-level retail jobs that involve stocking shelves and being able to interpret a planogram—even if they aren't fashion related, at first. It can be easy to find merchandising jobs, even in a small town, and the skills you pick up there will carry into fashion merchandising jobs. Visual merchandisers often choose to go on to become buyers, so you can easily continue your career in fashion.

Is this visual merchandiser hanging this dress up or removing it from the rack? To answer this question, consider whether or not this piece fits in with the overall color scheme (or tells a similar "color story") as the other pieces on the rack.

FASHION BUYER PRACTICE

Have you noticed how sometimes one person within a school (or even a small group of friends) comes in one day with a new jacket, purse, or pair of shoes … and suddenly everyone is demanding to know where she got it? Within the next week, several girls are suddenly wearing the same thing. You'll see this behavior on Instagram as well—sometimes viewers are so rabid to know where a garment comes from, they don't even bother being polite about it.

Just for fun, see if you can predict which of your friends might snap up a new trend. Come in with something new and make sure everyone sees it. Subtly sing the praises of your new shoes; make sure you tell everyone where you got them. (Bonus points if they're on sale—people love to buy things that are on sale.) Now sit back and wait. Do any of your friends buy the same thing? If so, you just successfully acted as a "buyer," in a small way. Do other people within your group of friends, or even within your school, buy them?

Take a good look at the usual style of these people. Does this new purchase seem logical for them and fit in with their personal styles?

SALARY EXPECTATIONS

The salary for fashion buyers varies. For updated salary information, refer to the Bureau of Labor Statistics website.

CAREER OUTLOOK

Demand for fashion buyers is currently on the rise, but this is a job you may need to relocate for—the headquarters of most retail stores and clothing companies are located in large cities.

FOR MORE INFORMATION

BOOKS

Clodfelter, Richard. *Retail Buying: From Basics to Fashion*. New York, NY: Fairchild, 2013.
Step-by-step instructions take you through the process of buying, creating merchandising plans, and understanding your clients.

Mathis, Karen. *Fashion Buyer*. San Diego, CA: Netsales & Arts, 2012.
Written by a long-time retail fashionista who eventually opened her own shop, this book covers everything from interview tips to what apps to use when working.

Shaw, David, and Dimitri Koumbis. *Fashion Buying: From Trend Forecasting to Shop Floor*. New York, NY: Fairchild, 2013.
Five succinct chapters teach you the basics of recognizing trends, making wise purchases, budgeting, and more.

ORGANIZATIONS

Association for Retail Environments
440 N. Wells Street, Suite 740
Chicago, IL 60654
Website: http://www.retailenvironments.org
Dedicated to "enhancing the total shopper experience,"
 this association publishes educational information
 and also sponsors industry awards.

National Association of Retail Buyers
440 N. Wells Street, Suite 740
Chicago, IL 60654
Website: http://www.narbuyers.org/17/home-page
 -narb.htm
This group is "dedicated to developing the careers and
 education of its members." Check out their website for
 events and sponsorship opportunities.

WEBSITES

Because of the changing nature of internet links, Rosen
Publishing has developed an online list of websites
related to the subject of this book. This site is updated
regularly. Please use this link to access this list:

http://www.rosenlinks.com/CCWC/fash

GLOSSARY

ANGEL INVESTORS Individuals who invest money in the early stages of a start-up.

BARRIER TO ENTRY How difficult or easy it is to get into a field. For example, the barrier to entry for being a doctor is high. The barrier to entry for being a cashier is low.

CLIPS Well-polished writing samples that showcase your talent and range, which you can send to a prospective employer.

COLLABORATION A group working together to create something.

CONSIGNMENT When you bring your products to a store under the understanding that they will pay you for what sells and return unsold products.

COUTURE The business of making and selling fashionable women's clothing.

EN VOGUE Also "in vogue," meaning in current fashion or style.

FLOORSET When a retail store rearranges all their displays, rotates their stock, and puts out the newest shipment of styles.

HAUTE COUTURE High-quality, very expensive, and fashionable articles of clothing that are made to order.

IT GIRL A young woman who has achieved celebrity status because of her socialite lifestyle.

LINESHEET A piece of paper that contains important information about your company and products, meant to entice a sale.

LOCAL RAG Local newspaper, sometimes used in a negative sense.

LOOKBOOK A collection of photographs that showcases a designer's new collection.

NICHE A specialized part of a market.

PITCH A quick summary or teaser meant to persuade someone to purchase your article.

PLATFORM Your combined social media presence.

PORTFOLIO A collection of your photos, writing samples, designs, or other work. Sometimes print and sometimes hosted on the web, a portfolio helps you show your talents to future employers, collaborators, and buyers.

PRÊT-À-PORTER The French term for ready-to-wear fashion.

READY-TO-WEAR "Off the rack" fashion that is made for the general public.

RELEASE FORMS Forms that acts to terminate any liability between the releasor and releasee.

BIBLIOGRAPHY

Beckett, Nicole. *The Fantabulous Girl's Guide to Wardrobe Styling: How to Break into the Fashion & Entertainment Industry*. Amazon Digital Services, 2015.

Clodfelter, Richard. *Retail Buying: From Basics to Fashions*. New York, NY: Fairchild Publications, 2003.

Freer, Alison. *How to Get Dressed: A Costume Designer's Secrets for Making Your Clothes Look, Fit, and Feel Amazing*. Emeryville, CA: Ten Speed, 2015.

Goss, Judy. *Break into Modeling for Under $20*. New York, NY: St. Martin's Griffin, 2008.

Hayward, Sarah. *Fashion Blogging: How to Become a Superstar Fashion Blogger*. Lion Day, 2015.

Lane, R. C. *The Model's Bible*. CreateSpace, 2013.

Mathis, Karen. *Fashion Buyer*. San Diego, CA: Netsales & Arts, 2012.

Shaw, David, and Dimitri Koumbis. *Fashion Buying: From Trend Forecasting to Shop Floor*. New York, NY: Fairchild, 2013.

Sigel, Eliot. *Photographing Women: 1,000 Poses*. Berkeley, CA: Peachpit, 2012.

Stewart, Briana, and Brian Cliette. *Clothing Line Start-up Secrets: How to Start and Grow a Successful Clothing Line*. CreateSpace, 2014.

Swanson, Kristen K., and Judith C. Everett. *Writing for the Fashion Business*. New York, NY: Fairchild, 2008.

INDEX

ABOUT THE AUTHOR

Alison Downs is a writer and editor living in the greater New York City area. A graduate of Goddard College and Southern New Hampshire University (where she received her BFA in creative writing and her MA in English, respectively), she has had a lingering interest in fashion ever since she received a Fashion Plate light box as a child. Her current style icons are Audrey Hepburn and Kate Middleton. Find her on Twitter @alison_face and on the web at http://www.alisondowns.org.

PHOTO CREDITS:

Cover, p. 3 S_L/Shutterstock.com; 6–7 lev radin/ Shutterstock.com; pp. 10–11 Stokkete/Shutterstock .com; pp. 12–13 mimagephotography/Shutterstock .com; p. 15 Evan Lorne/Shutterstock.com; pp. 22–23 Andre Luiz Moreira/Shutterstock.com; pp. 24–25 © Scott Bairstow/Alamy Stock Photo; p. 27 bikeriderlondon/ Shutterstock.com; pp. 34–35 © iStockphoto.com/ andresr; p. 36 EQRoy/Shutterstock .com; p. 39 © Bob Daemmrich/Alamy Stock Photo; p. 44 © Everett Collection Inc/Alamy Stock Photo; p. 46 © picturelibrary/Alamy Stock Photo; pp. 48–49 Blend Images/Shutterstock.com; pp. 54–55 sergey causelove/